Calm
color by
numbers

Calm
color by numbers

David Woodroffe

SIRIUS

SIRIUS

This edition published in 2021 by Sirius Publishing, a division of
Arcturus Publishing Limited,
26/27 Bickels Yard, 151–153 Bermondsey Street,
London SE1 3HA

ISBN: 978-1-83940-732-1
CH004923NT
Supplier 29, Date 0621, Print run 11808

Printed in China

INTRODUCTION

Coloring is a fantastic way to unwind and focus your mind, and this book of calming color-by-number images has been designed to do just that. The collection includes animals and landscapes, decorative patterns, optical illusions, and images inspired by art, dance and meditation.

Spend a little time matching your colored pencils to the colors in the key – you can even label each one with a number to make things easier. Then choose an image and carefully start to build up the color, taking your time over the detail and small color areas. The image will slowly start to come together and you should find the process of coloring itself a relaxing escape from the pressures of the everyday.

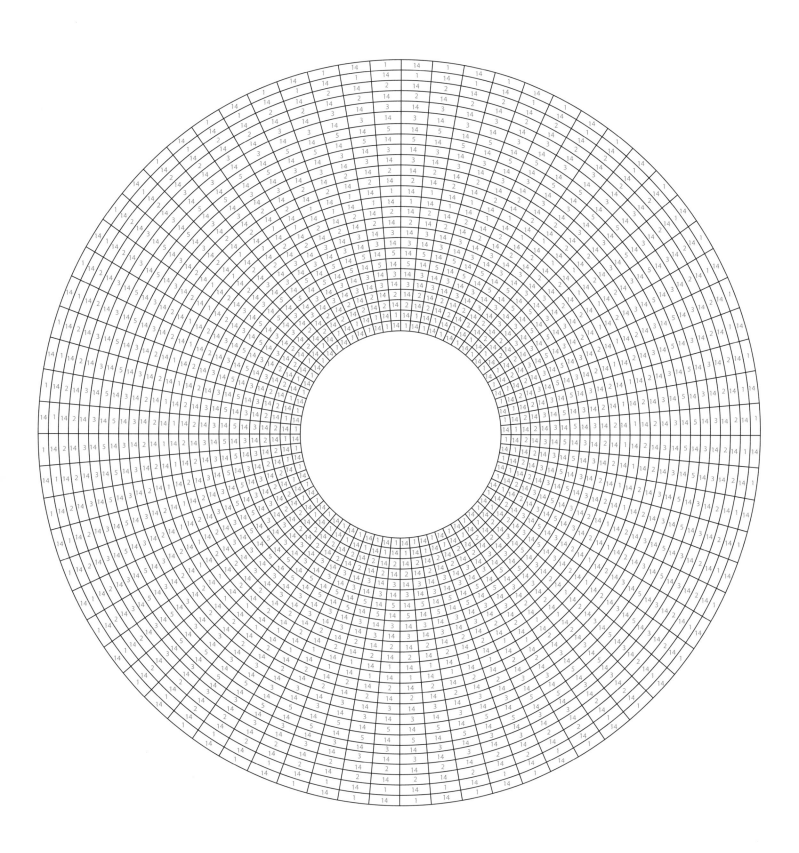

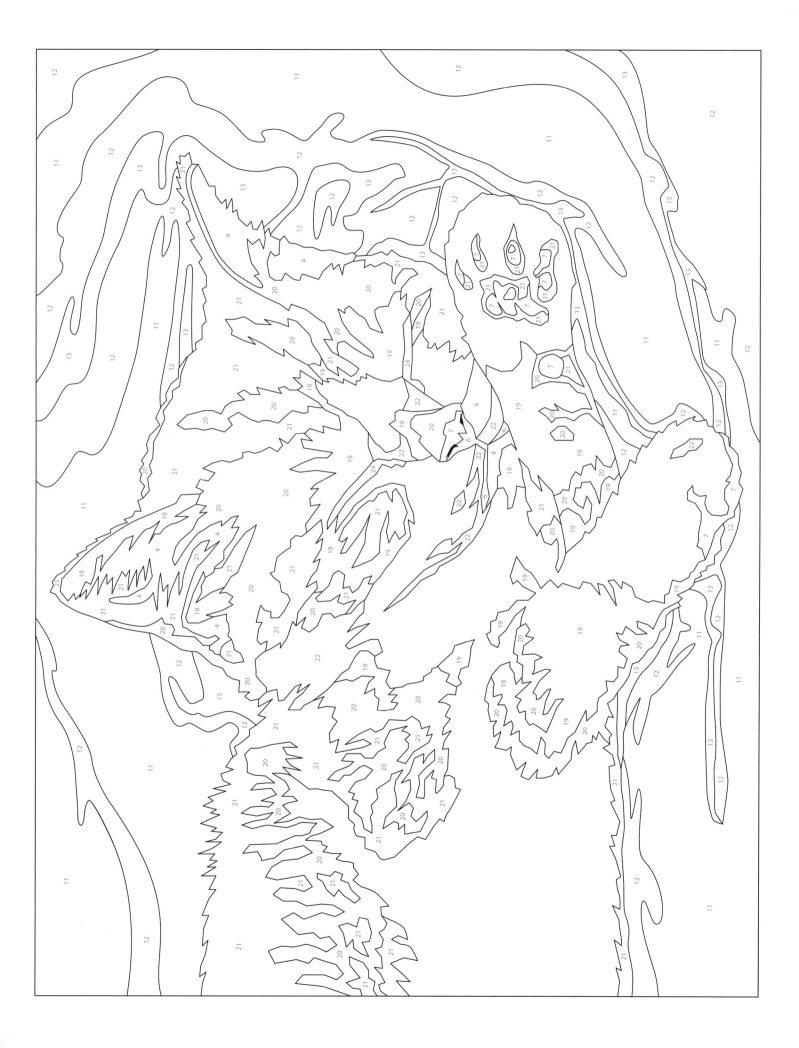

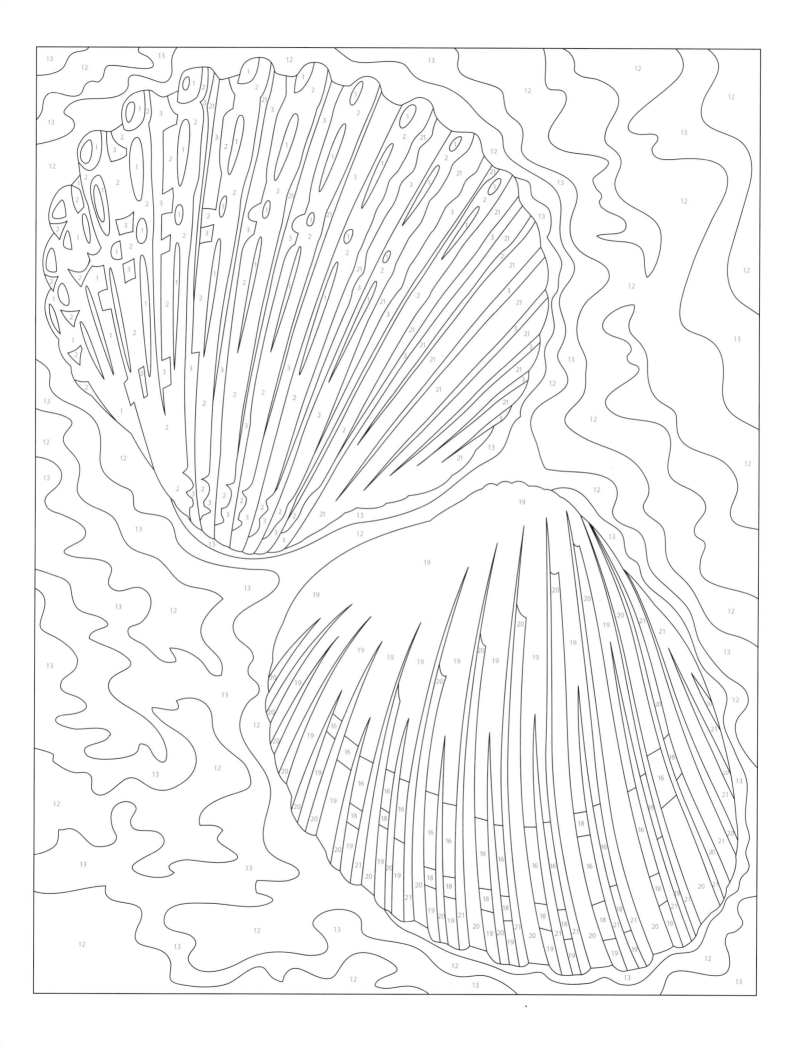